AF597877

Also by Spencer Selby:

Instar (SINK, 1989)
Barricade (Paradigm Press, 1990)
Stigma (Score, 1990)
House of Before (Poets and Poets, 1991)
Sound Off (Detour Press, 1993)
Malleable Cast (Generator, 1995)

NO ISLAND

NO ISLAND

Spencer Selby

Drogue Press New York 1995

Works from *No Island* have appeared in *Anabasis* (The Love Project), *Antenym*, *Atelier*, *B City*, *Bughouse*, *Caliban*, *Cathay*, *Collectif Reparation de Poesie* (Canada), *Cyanosis*, *Denver Quarterly*, *Die Young*, *Ergo*, *First Intensity*, *First Offense* (U.K.), *fragmente* (U.K.), *Garuda* (U.K.), *House Organ*, *Indefinite Space*, *Interruptions*, *Intimacy* (U.K.), *Juxta*, *Lost and Found Times*, *MOHS* (France), *New American Writing*, *Oasis* (U.K.), *Object Permanence* (U.K.), *Poetics Briefs*, *Ramraid Exraordinaire* (U.K.), *Shearsman* (U.K.), *Sivullinen* (Finland), *Spinne* (Germany), *Talisman*, *Terrible Work* (U.K.), *3 X 4* (U.K.), *TO* and *Turbulence*; in the anthologies *The Gertrude Stein Awards: 1994-1995* (ed. D. Messerli, Sun and Moon Press) and *Primary Trouble* (ed. J. Donahue, E. Foster and L. Schwartz, Talisman House); and in a chapbook *Frontier* (Lingua Blanca, Esbo, Finland). The author is grateful to the editors of all these publications.

Published by Drogue Press
P.O. Box 1157, Cooper Station, New York, NY 10276

Designed and typeset by Spencer Selby

Printed in the USA by McNaughton and Gunn

ISBN 0-9628456-7-1

CONTENTS

THE SPREAD

Who goes beyond appearance
is a searcher after.
Head through adamantine vault,
darkness without bottom,
living theater perfect spell
perpetrated upon an exquisite
harmony of contradictions.

Revelation challenge to accept
intercourse that hid itself
under an image of the sacred
warning and promise
whose answer is to veil both terror
and fascination, to bind the world
to something previously divided.

There stands judgment,
just like two knobs formulated
in triumphant paradox.
Partners in a dialogue,
pairs of concepts defining
a division brought to life
by each experience.

To cut something in two
is the mark of a ritual passing
from one state to another.
Because it is so fateful
we cannot help noticing
the space cut off from roots
we used to worship.

A process like a voyage
appears somehow to grapple
with a statement of purpose
that suddenly becomes inadequate.
One moment it's all there
while the next embraces shadows
we can hardly imagine.

Something said against a story
moves uneasily between extremes
of high-pitched voices and
faces on a wall made contemporary
by aspects of a positive negative
presented in a series
of unacknowledged events.

Endless products illustrate
what happens when this problem
becomes more direct. Looking
outward at a world we never made
creates a window of tyranny.
How we feel about the damage
pushes in two directions at once.

CREVICE

Content opening
in keeping something larger
denotes inward stain.

So slow when past the threshold
assimilated back to view
a dark named alternate silence.

Have measure attentive in the keyhole
straight preverbal made present
in the time of the poem's argument
with words that stand for immediate.

Tears think twice around this
unacknowledged paradox,
resemble pursue diverse strategy
to get things said against what is missing
from the bottom upwards.

Float vengeance needs pronouncing
worldly bones in the catastrophic period
altered not enough.
Memorial of burned feet dredges up
clashing secrets at the outer reaches of
looking differently at the evidence.

Written state speaks grand permission
partly lost in a forest or jungle.
Desperate raining tears
from untoward strength that thought to
exist apart and love every current
mode of address.

Temptation situates here
whose piercing thought breaks off
in midstream which has no need
of something visible.

Wishborn subject taking a chance
with tomorrow's inability
to separate life from an ancient problem.
Naked matter home a threat
for the innocent victim standing in a
shadow I think about constantly.

Saying I do and I don't
in relation to language surrounded
with the infinite.

A world of good examples
depending on what used to be irrelevant.
Speech search temple of darkness
so much satisfied by an outside
embryonic experience.

Full force burning pale
as the beauty which may or may not
fit this landscape
will never look the same.

Words I imagine being still
from going dead to life of the answer
where forgotten daylight
keeps things moving in a way
that doesn't show itself till the end.

LITURA

Negative word bypass
no true better than what is said
or where it is when time changed
an unbecoming wish

Since left a limited relation
all physical process
due to separate chances made
that amount of character the same

Point of object to her
must be part of a natural
language and vision mistaken for
lips sealed just as well

With no pain towards
critical insight
of three-fold circumstance wherein
nothing would go down below

With every attempt would she
anticipate the logic which sustains
an overrated formula
by normal warlike skill

Embarrassed before that source
when the screen of mind
must circumvent some religious finding
in the counterweight on the left

Best exit next pleasure
at her devastating compulsion
would have centered on some curious
vessel exploded from without

Undergoes meaning handled with
new part the point identified
no longer and in constant light of
current narrative fault

Said she knew it but didn't belong
said another insight
held both feet together
with material that was still unfair

Sure enough wrote down
relentless disturbing judgment
kept away from the glass
which separates day from night

Followed the same road
in time for removal of a memory
that made her keep coming back
for an accident she loved so much

Could see then couldn't
repetition cause the tangled rescue
accepted on one side
but moving forward on another

Take back what's important
in between happy sad curtailment
of all the current figures
who don't believe her name

Question conscious value
as if perhaps she dropped everything
just to save what might be growing
in her heart.

THE FOLLOWING *for SE*

1.

I suppose I understand at best
throughout work based on a root
respect for word method combinations.

Beginning of the above immediately
divides into fear and cause result.
Could be temerity between the city

circle squared with resultant stasis.
What follows fruition ended by
boldness at the corner verging on

next step daylight made out to be
black. A cloudy darkness gathering
falling crystalline bed, equally

sleeping and childbirth behung.
Suspended or resurrected hue of man,
both lunatic and essence in every poem.

I read this as a microcosm within the
larger noon-day transmuted into gold,
an implication that will last

as long as it is voicing prophet
telling token to keep moving through
the one thing common we now have.

2.

Context stream shows an alertness
to shifts implicit in language.

Nothing more final than abiding
hands on a quest within relational

and attending sets of myth.
Numen sentences extended into

flux of later lushness being proposed.
Divinity in a word, unfolding gnosis

seeing itself in action that involves
restoring sense to a phantom.

3.

Interlocking passage employed
without immediate margins.

Take off from precisely that point
in a difficult perception.

Hermetic flower which absents
an ethos of likewise crossing.

Lips, hair and cylinders going on
a telling yet gathered.

4.

Energies here are contentious surface,
lyric aspect, fulfillment light ascensions not
for the sake of beauty alone.

Their primacy is to actualize potencies
that inhere within matter, sounding language
commensurate with weight.

Referents strike primary as purpose bind,
phase of being able joining desire that evokes
and engages the world.

A kind of marriage reveals exactly those forms
bursting back into syntax, tells meaning
I believe is real world other.

Not simply a twin but a substantive third
by which the work makes intersections and
multiple naming that opens

itself across the barriers of fluent speech,
scoring music stuck along the lines of what's
intended as a whole.

TREATMENT

Blink of an eyelid calling forth
a different meaning
as response to prevailing forces.

The subject taken by surprise,
covering proof against behavior
we have glorified in dreams

that exist only where there is
strife, violence and consumption.
In every quarter we find

continual counterpoint between
the uproar and containment of
a battle that never changed anyone.

The full range of choices has failed
in its movement through a vacuum
that by now is quite notorious.

Well I know all about it,
they will tell you, and then
the world grows dark with reasons

which are used to separate this part
of the story from almost everything.
To fight for more and settle for less

is the way we've come, not dead
but sleeping with shadows spilling
from deep inside the labyrinth.

Play the game don't play the game,
all the same it had to happen.
The way of action got stuck

on the path of least resistance.
All roads led to a tunnel in the
middle of something obvious.

Thwarting minds to keep in view
a question streaming back
from here and now.

THE UNINVITED

1.

Inability to change in the face of
advance design dept.
A course we oppose to accept
by asking questions
based on long experience.

Things that didn't happen
with their pockets full of it.
A birthday party in a hurry.
A peepshow running out of luck.

2.

Same function which the upright
patient misses.
Tension induced by problems
that don't expect an answer
from people who ought to know better.

Impossible thing ever to stop
layer after layer sliding down
contiguous memory
without getting caught.

3.

Surroundings not well liked
for excess population.
New wrinkles that perhaps
give up the ghost
learned from wrong examples.

Difficult Obdurate Conveyance
Unlikely Belief Appointment
Motive that lies in any ocean
you might cover on your way to work.

4.

Kills time by illegible keyhole
that doesn't cost a fortune.
Agitator of language
astounded but not swallowed.

Recent portrait
waiting for an echo
being dried in the sun
by mistake of something else.

5.

Revolving door so easily forgotten.
Mouthful bad enough in fashion.
More beautiful through defeat
as opposed to domination.

Unknown territory seemingly content
but not really.
Habit knowledge expressing anomaly
only on the way out.

6.

Window bars meaning in the shadow
of an unfinished attempt.
Negotiation too real to be completed.
Arrangement showing details
which are stuck between the birth

and death of here and there,
the top and bottom of a world
that seems so often
like an earthquake waiting to happen.

7.

Mother of Mischief.
Father of Want.
Experience more potent
than thought.

Expressive in a way that suffers
from being overdressed.
Verbalized by almost everyone
from a point where they can't give up.

DISCOVERY *for JR*

A suspicious dark suit
that in this age of low culture
will be permitted to do nothing else.

Man in religious photograph
waving at a serpent
on the edge of poor attention.

Primitive light source
in the left hand of a poet
who doesn't know how to write.

Mythology as discipline for response.
Brutal environment lacking love
to the degree of being crippled.

Movement stolen back
in the big Paris church
still exhausted by a hidden memory.

Colors everywhere around the neck.
Experience glorified
without an excuse for present meaning.

Subject author saying the truth
did other things on the bridge
created by a demolition expert.

No one nowhere ever since,
like discovery of modern
ship sinks every minute.

Ditto voice illuminated night
developed brain to hinder
a much better tragedy than this.

MEAN

Fierce equivalent
from worlds of light within

a framework that is governed by
where to have supply of creation.

Unknown breathless counterpart
in the history of human speech.

Massive drama of the foreign land
that comes to dwell here.

Situation full of danger,
written in a different sense,

succumbing to a value
left over from what was lost.

+

Riddled system, demonic entity
charged with personal significance.

Compulsive force rather than a unity
to which unredeemed life might defer.

Time perspective as a source of anguish
matched only by the terror which

comes in the middle of one
further psychological turn.

Given a name between the realm
of one kind of darkness and another.

Between the current outpost
and a future we don't need.

RELIC

I find the whole idea crystallized out of
talking about denominator vs. society
missionary appeal similar to
the cooling so few people have felt
that serves as only a relic
can understand.

Bizarre movement toward darkness
dreaming night can pass through
what's motivating purpose and
tribulation trying so hard
to wake everyone up.

Spoken language far older
when I think to say I've got
the story wrong.

Not signify a kind of mental field
over and above experience
taken with water distilled from or
tapping into diurnal residence
of high-speed illusion of control
and dominance.

Better concrete surface can't see
through a metaphor stretched in being
stared at on that royal road I find
meets current vision filling the void
between one body and another.

Auric field curiously designed
before trading reality as
someone else's art.
Crude spark necessary by
dissolving line of influence
that is wrong about
what tomorrow must give up.

Part of people not explored
like colorless tasteless liquid
spreads far and wide
with childhood written on
clumsy material.

The other part grown tired of
survival seems a word like
cobweb or payload
makes the inner search fall flat.

For this I know and cannot question:
words as things is wonderful
only in detail that gets lost
in cold weather remove
brought back by quirky music.

The snow comes down under a single
cloud on the brink of motion.
My lips turn serious
and then it takes all winter
to admit the question changed
while I was out.

KAFKA-LIKE RESPONSE *for SM*

whose modus questions a power relationship
over the very act of asking.

Expectation light of inherent violence
by way of think genre through determination.

Same issue extent to which unity
should be taken as cautionary knowledge.

Vectors that provide against work always
produced with profound disruption awareness

invested into considering the way back to
the value of so much negation.

Role demanded by motives ignored or subverted.
Rather different recently read plot in which

certain qualities determined phrasing that's
returned to a psychic contract with the reader.

Ability to enter and destroy prose not prose
agreement with the sites of meaning.

Warrant political in the sense that already is
marginalized on the edge of this claim.

Certainly it would be refreshing to promote
an exploratory rather than canonic norm,

to realize validation in the ongoing struggle
that repudiates this hugely disparate cogency

of cultural indicators and habits of reading.
Deliberate foliage that speaks its own advance

instead of seeing people agree with
a further mistake of language and philosophy.

Aspect quoted passage of the child double
of the word, writing itself clear to a level

identified as marks of being whilst wishing
to decentre the subject I'm on.

CLOSE

be held close
in an ordinary piece of

raindrops inside the shadow

exact course to one another
that looked like
vertical menacing

caught on a stone-faced word
deserted line may surface
if a better critic
talks about what happened

safe as it appears
but in reality has another origin

deeper than their lives
accurate to present prophecy

strike benefit through glass
justified in assuming
false promises will not be able
to change direction

look close endangered earth

mass stop halfway
payment foolish boundary
authentic imaginary
dead flower shape and sequence

entered a point in the story of

head downward
examination all over
play faculty to itself deceptive

wrong for believing
a world in love with that

NEWS

News of your dilemma dropped names
in accordance with each part played
in the process of changing into
something left unsaid.

Inside and out was certain
to make you nervous when so many
had decided not to spread themselves
where they weren't wanted.

One target too many became
the only thing that people noticed
when you entered the room.
In the corner unacknowledged

a hidden passage came and went
before the truth of your experience
could look up from its newspaper
and make itself known.

Composite portraits fell apart
when critical reaction left without
saying a word about the circumstance
of your victory within defeat.

More than that and less
is where you've been while changing
costumes and getting difficult
from then to now.

The only way you'll fill in the blank
is cutting across the boundary
of an unsympathetic response.
Bridge to be a verdict

talking about the incapacity of words
to say what they've created,
an iridescent light spread mostly
forward and back,

filling a need down below
that starts a new world every minute,
taking untold present wonder
for a loss.

MUTATION STOPS *for CL*

Time does what you want,
dimensional fact serious enough
wearing certain choices
combined with patience of two
planetary curves, pretense
for years in banishment,
abundantly activated
light color episodes
all thought as yet another
good volunteer friendship
stuck behind temerity to know.

+

Expectation is looking after
denial outshining mainly the thing
convergent upon irreversible
shipwrecked memory, or perhaps
songs so stretching forth
without within pronounced
hollow of rock, more resplendent
world outfit made under
research fit to be tied.

+

Address faced down upon
the lips of dark conjunction.
Trenchant teachings rearrange
same deft landscape
finally won through strategy
in lieu of that approach.
Sound and sense stagger words
they cannot leave alone
in a world produced by persuasion
standing pat because
no metaphor would work as well.

+

Which lowdown readable earth
endured a safe escort,
better nature subject
fallen unto description
without doubt stolen from
experience so struggle can
discern one common heap
waiting for a workproof death,
claimed to cleanse the future
of vision we no longer resolve.

+

Rising through divided love,
grown like a poison desire
removed from sight,
played for too much time
to come until it seems
tomorrow doth change
an influence shaken from
the massive pulse of life
which outcomes defer.

+

Twin mistakes run backwards
through mile after mile
of circumstantial evidence.
Said reports keep bitter
pangs of conscience at bay,
at length returning unknowable
solitude to that laughter
which surpasses everything
we've come to associate
with yesterday's results.

+

Not remembered by fallen
equilibrium, not sufficient
as a large mirror operating
in the very depths reduced
so easily to pseudo capacity.
Filled up with discourse
then thrown out where
the world couldn't be
more curious or less
practical if it tried.

+

So spoke the guide
taken for a ride
with some such evolution
trailing far behind.
Or maybe we were wrong
and new nature forms
counterfeit openings
into fluid magnetic targets
we can't catch up with
during the night.

+

Tears stream forth no differently
than when those words first
came to mean something
you don't dare admit today.
Meanings are scattered
to punish the deep foundation
seeking passage from that
very source, moving outside
just about everything
you think might still be hovering
on both sides of a heart.

+

Secondary partition as evasive
document, eyes and legs reacting
to a face you liken to divine
departure of a dream betrayed
by a faulty use of freedom
in everyday life. Hard cold
facts working overtime,
doing what they like
in a space we can't hardly
get along without.

+

Up the long road and then
back down, pressing hard upon
diversions so well disposed
toward chemistry that keeps
time interwoven with travelers
whose knowledge of each departure
won't stay put.

+

True dead wormwood of affliction,
encompassing removal
of this and that suit of armor,
scattering the dialogue
which comes much later and now
is mainly shown to be inadequate,
turning over a chunk of tomorrow
and wiping it off.

ENDURANCE

eyes memory gaping
suspect falls

eating habit
direct figure

work of a lifetime
art embedded nonverbal

shaft of sun
road at night
held necessary to question

sense of common bond
the name the voice
a world was made from

nowhere work it every day
billions and billions
star in a sense
distance another

far across desert
space approach
avoidance approach

green from red
wrong from center
split by thunder natural not
the wound or after

suspect cold at the window
future erase the given

come here liquid
import zero fashion
danger capital without

CRAFT

Sounds the deathknell preeminent
phase-out between beliefs.
Divergent installed on a corpse,
escape revolt passage defeating claims
absorbed by zero silence.

Desire involved spectrum to the last
unpopular effective discourse.
Pure protest or poisonous refusal,
valid margin or X closed off diagnosis
that the patient always sought.

Locked here in situ
to operate the phantom limb,
attack so radical endemic character,
debate resource advance against reality,
show victim of history, flesh and
weapons about to be shed.

Such would be our logic
using a self-consuming model
instead of a threat. Strange present
we have now, expressing exhaustion
reflection profusion throughout
an entire economy.

Dark meaning as a miracle
anticipated and done in by device.
Joint vectors that generate more space
in the desert frame withdrawal
from both directions at once.

Search program for an end for
perception positive afterlife career.
Sign commerce held hostage
and embarrassed by an argument
no longer made.

Mark question means of difference,
cast shadow ruins against museum
performance, create deny
this culture whose development
is a myth.

STRAND

1.

What everybody knows
you say you don't, or else
the right as rain discovery
must have converted
the part of reason's task
we lost for love of meaning
in the meantime, fighting
over who to believe and
what to avoid and where
to unburden ourselves next.

2.

Not knowing brought knowledge
that cried aloud.
Through every second breath
the blades of your instruction
keep horizons separated
from a life stocked with
readouts and answers,
proving false values
by conversational comparison.

3.

Experience as usual
the old tent you might
stumble upon as no other.
The urge to minimize thought
is held inside that veiled request
which must have forgotten why
you entered so easily
and ran straight up the pole.

SO LONG

Life again set off
by chatter
ring around it rushing
perverse material
defended like it was a hymn

Press seed charge from
roots that narrow
soft blow begging brightness
weary intimate
voice of age in advance

Together with the only
world I know for certain
death
flower petal eros nature
down the appetite I'm hearing
with my head

I've seen black eye
to carry habit
look nothing break loose
total be granted
more work fall apart
shadow I promoted

Now years after
there is plenty earth moaning
at my embrace hidden in
shades of dramatic
give it a chance

Instincts reawaken
what I didn't think
was action needs quiet
blood trail and damage
of a very rare moment

No silence touches remorse
as larval quality
no tangent temporal feeling
remains in the past
I point toward in my
strung out wish

MOIRA

Swelling her demand
achieved first privilege
then end of upwards
to engulf fire in one frame.

Stuck motion slipped eye
in tomorrow's descent.
Dead hallway hurt body
under meanwhile
on the body's account.

Truly burden head and tail
coiled around without measure.
Fabric so much beneath extremes,
smashed and driven
at the deepest level.

Moonlight saying it didn't happen
because we weren't able.
Blood in the mouth perhaps to swim
in what can only be unanswered.
Sole purpose, compelling force
removed from all our actions.

Flesh dream made happy
by the troublesome present.
Close held matter around
which line of ignorance.

Bomb definition, rap voice
crossing naked surface
patch of street or hands thrown up
like more excessive
by the time we can not help.

VENDETTA

Money mind castle broods on approach of death. Shady financial wants to put off research found in a job-lot library by a writer of raw guts. The secret has been discovered but there is a catch. To live must reconcile animal enjoyment that completes a grim satire on the age and possibilities outflowing this.

No time once said tomorrow is not lying about a place named eternal. Modern mythology covering language swathed with ropes and daubs. Accomplished actuality through device of one order lying behind another. Zone of import both extended and limited as to action it deserves.

Labyrinthine suggests pursuit despite alternative blotted out by list of enemies. Torrid decay giving sermons in jungle clearings. Mass state turned harrowing from nowhere. Passionate referred glory to be imperfect curse of hindsight art.

Success struggle occupying people's minds, selling out popular contest now overtaken with a sense of nervous youth. Report on dialogue felt moving against the bridge which is formidable. Willingness to speak and turn the book whose own great fall rises again, plays second finger beneath the city which is her husband.

Treadmill music and light dark corridors of sleep. Last decade nature era, probably round about the first world divided. Deep relationship other external, recorded and echoed by many who lived through the war against politics closely examined. Promise which defied conventions and cemented travel through far greater knowledge remaining in doubt.

Real fiction understood or formulated who makes the chase go well. Certain meaning heads off more and more on the outskirts of human thought. Original cast out future resource killed by time of memory whose subject is at a loss.

Denies problems by placing a dry epilogue in all work of good. Becomes effective as various strands woven apart from dissolution and a violent principle that counts backwards as a way between poverty and avoidance of the West.

Does the mirror trick for matter appropriate to a family haunted by God. Hound of Heaven pursuing the entrance to improbable seduction and so on. Charm portraits in shadow of such desire says what body is causing trouble no matter what.

Accent pointed at immemorial dark closed world that is sustained by tradition. Lord of gestures, complicated discharge scrubbers, predestined sacerdotal legs off burning killing father mad remains to offset swimming in a sea of red.

Almost present, like single bad choice wants but cannot move around the name which brings it. Deliberate diabolic party outside is thrown into weakness and flaws which are growing in all of us. Contemporary symptomatic free will mess that is never total. Martyr victim story and logic nailed beyond regret.

Time and place, sweat and rain, unsure convert, unwise vehicle taken differently as always happens with vow and not report communion. Loving sacrilege implied by a wrong excitement. Condemned message from an excess of motive that is drawing pressure from above.

Full face forward and in future power morality. High command not enamored of human decency. Two extremes before attack shows marriage of typical Americans. Skin, muscle and nerves' desire to range importance with a device borrowed from sexual preoccupation. Naked leaving dead behind impulse exhausted while being driven by another myth.

Form called negative to conform with rejection of the gods' last wish. Less at home servant that still needs the status of a word like truth. Disruption taken as a small good-hearted protest against society, a clown's temper not found in children who have enough rest.

DRUM

Inward light leaving self-evident trace
of memory outside the window.

Head shone in sky, impervious moment
of building horizon to alter the dark
tempest curse I have spent my
life crossing over.

Sidelong breath
uprooting strength of reflection.
Ocean stirred on the way
by overflowing today's narrow standard.

Said lucid touch before the body
extends its fire on parallel of obvious,
on words I have, key I have not
drawn forth, put in context, made
transparent, dark, dangerous and mean.

Enemy found this more closely
deep past desert now returning
sure as dare compare itself to you
who are the way my spirit has fallen.

Ground to ground of familiar support,
conscious whole point spread out in
book and dialogue, reflex likely
on the edge of a flood I have no end of.

Fluid passage true for both,
terror and delight, joy and sorrow
carried by what is felt beyond
the current framework.

Formal vital sense of learning
influence you have given me,
stirred up working clay
mountain ridge pressure
open land so far from all this
fear, greed and prejudice.

Living thing I know in my childhood
which I use against the speaking
part of both, world skin at the
written side of death that you must
always read back to me.

Made self poem uncomfortably large,
world under ice as if the fringes
are in remission, now fragments
more complex by definition.

Charm circle all the way
when we are together.
Come to finish like meaning,
rescue thought in the station
where it's political.

Talks big but not through
surface center till we
stand alone and look outside as one.

DRAW

All seldom song
words like frank centrifugal
page innocent where there is
no vantage stolen
for the rest

Light there onward as defense
threaten ground via distance
play the trace
to hold no less this epoch
founded acute rough motion
around the head of it

Show again familiar
force capital content
grown from sea of what
we didn't take into our bed
so immediate

Make ring true the only
character brought back to be
what we are in liberty
struck by sense of
wilderness absorbed

The way we climb and get lost
the way tomorrow affects
our crowning voice
with its own thick air for
trade in open defiance
heading south

WHAT FOR

Passage rarified
does not lead a certain prejudice
from belaboring what's important.
Either by land or by ice
the story gets sidetracked.

Quality of remoteness,
memory of severance,
transient awareness to distinguish
between suffering and the perilous
plunge from a world of static hope.

Floor to ceiling mirror
given and then rejected by all who've
lost their substitute for innocence.
Written in blood by a reckless
groping for personal advantage.

Taken for granted beyond limits
mistaken for reality.
Released across the country
by a crooked instinct that was
never more appropriate.

Brought down in the current
counterpoint yawning ever wider
through an eruption of fire
burning the social body
with nothing but failed truth.

UPPER MIDDLE

Native solitude
combat negotiable sleep or death.

I went out so daring
shrank back climbing range
trance perfect smile
pilot me direction dizzy
produce gift of shrewd overlapping.

Self courage in the world
play the part land here
bubbles with signs, counsels
prayers, admonitions arising from
the nothingness I remember incorrectly.

Face all along stratum of hardness.
Say deliberate but mean mad itinerant
streets and streets give shadow of
cement linear I mistake as indecent
as a natural function.

I cannot stop or move around
city stench mood held responsible
headless race of machines.
I spend my life shining black
to avoid blue and step by step
to the voice behind me saying
what remains of power enigma.

Circumstance enchanting articles
blocked by a staircase
pervading atmosphere of doubt.
Talk in houses in appointed places
funny familiar incessant character
manufactured by means last discovered
for a loud and lengthy analysis.

Prison yard dubbed a garden
rent creature limited percentage
taking a hand in the bandit premium.
Sweep floor furniture surrounding
commonplace righteous emphatic
rather than residue of the origin
I do not believe in.

Your soul it says belongs at the end
must listen by transition logic
arrest the former grievance
pour out heart for having
appeal as a chosen authority.

Issue police detail damage
receive the fate rendered breathless
show picture belonging failed obvious.

Eye-sore value dark upon the landscape
baffle haunting vital spoken
descriptive merciless.

Tower brave the wealth it covers
saturate multitude reason for homeless
crowd the evidence take exception
savage principle restore ability
that is my ticket home.

DEPOSIT

Dark flame entrance of the cave.
Soft spot like dream fallen that is
stuck for approval.
Self inflicted informant
of comprehension,
identified authentic because
normal use decoy isn't feeling it.

Unaware of the person standing
just inside, acoustic torture
of the real not far enough guise
plus incendiary impulse.

Debt I owe saturated of rats.
Time I have for trapdoor
blocked betrayal of innocence.
Talk I know is cheap unless I use
the name myth exploded of itself
in lifelong darkness.

So unlikely now the loose end
penetrating axis, lonely at the place
I imagine as motion carved from
underground silence.
Deep red glow that brings me
air and precious stone,
shell and shield encasing the light
I want to call endless.

Open my thought when I quit
coming down on the outside
of this sharp circle or that.
Illuminate mass grave absence,
profane exhausted appearance,
confounded contingent
tunnel of difference,
raising what I look for
in a friend.

TRIBUTE *for ARR*

Wilderness generated
building dimensional relief.
Whole life through moonlight,
survive mature grey black
most tragic reason in the world.

Fascinated namesake dialogue.
Branch thought claim blood,
warrant difference kingdom
reach to the water clear.

Goddess mountain sacrifice.
Condition period
healing realm no shortage,
difficult victim imagine
a woman back to earth.

Echo power in the middle
her body horizon flow.
Crude road visit various
animal address report.

Start up words by
the window museum she uses,
building account volunteer
wave in the western version.

Cloud liquid temple daring,
voice of the suspect
child narrative experience
peripheral archaic darkness
gathering prototype flood.

She lives alone where
people everywhere search.
Pictures from sleep introduce
mistake, regret and failure
to acknowledge a vehicle
swollen in her descent.

She drops the sky
before a more precise value,
before relief wind travel
approaches the perfect mask
of all biography.

Her hands pass over the target,
question empty surface,
shower mind by reservoir myth.

The day she works to push
reality against our preparation.
The feeling unknown courage,
future endless volume,
trouble smile rattle worship
close to the edge returning
what we can't remember
with our head.

COAT OF MAIL

Sombre whispering hints
hollow sound cut at the core
teeth rib close to dust in hand
breath raw power class
exhaled like a virus to remain
the far-flung starvation element

At school they said names were my goal
they said simple wonders don't work
for a life so easily forgotten
said didn't say brave influence
thought in turn sarcastic
dreaming library to swallow the script

Graven detail for a body I never wanted
for a rip-off story revenge in a family
almost total exhaust assembly
that didn't have a chance

More names like donuts' dialectic mass
response joining angle nature
language twisted in bad structure
broken chain plastic food for memory
taken with no expense

Part object refuse collection
movie mix wrong way no use
freedom of expression
doubt more real than this word
as current research direction

I'm never more alive than when I avoid
what so many closed eyes want to hear
I am thirsty with some great purpose
I can't take seriously when I
drink roots beyond proof and property
on the grey blue air before this moment
is suspended in a way I no longer
recognize as empty

Love flesh divine that wastes my time
in stones and circles failed by action
love voice untrue to make me learn
and forget why I'm here
love experience turning backwards
against my red-hot big mouth reason
love shadow now replacing
always sitting on the edge

What's that they say
and they are you me term display
in secret rain contagion
dream lustre sunlight fading
hammer glow long ache meaning
right or wrong a promise dying
so another can live

THE HUNGER *for SOM*

My hard vision as water veiled a curtain of sea, looked with anonymous all-around direction, groundless walls listening far beyond reach sound searching troubled memories, pounding swimming errant vantage came to a different account.

Human bones worship eyes like the crush of own weight, feeling out voyages on this sudden attitude current transmitted through lives loves words, mingling touching holding covering cold heat naked obstacle, being abandoned being caught by caress of volume absorbed and lost within the flow of movement desire more curious than thought.

I was thrown up on the rock. I was falling in between not knowing whether I would be strong enough on a layer of night. I was stuck, then turned the earth over on its side with such a stare flickering in the brilliant moment I want made quickly into a person I can share my solitude with.

A chance this was a chance like the imprint of her face. She moved as if aware and there was something ebbing back to sea. Her dress danced while the music was lost in the sound of arms of chairs of curtains around her neck. Machinery made imminent changed her luck, blinded her in a mirror past self. The people she had known the men she had loved following a script not revealed yet, shattering my mind caught looking at the mask of her face, the eyes I would see through if I were an idol like she is.

I wrote with the yielding of that woman. I carved her men's image, her eyes not men's of the poison of legends failed to engulf themselves. I wish to forget it was her that I challenged that night. The stones on her forehead, the sweetness burned with smoke of her perfume, the matter in frames and fire sense signal we hardly recognized. Her breath my reason, my pulse her motion, my apparent boyhood, her distantly remembered lust, my rockets my road my jungle swallowed messages given by her with a dark red smile on her lips.

The bed was floating, we were on it together moving slowly across. I was carrying so much weight for awhile and the cards fell out of her pocket. Then the ashes of something burned through both of us. The fever of her embrace, the thought of my body close to her body, the knowledge of some connection, some passage in the sun and light, the books and dream, the serpent shadow following both of us.

I speak to you whose beauty is mine if I let it be so, whose fire is mine if I am strong enough to nourish the illusion that there is no difference. Your golden thread leads from me to an enclosure where we slept one night. Your impression that the world is a ghost surrounding a window we both look out of. Your light that we undress in. Your voice from song of secret sentiment. Your choice to become what you are not. Your fears that are perfectly uncertain. Your love soon enough excluded from the passions we can't remember.

It will be me if you are lost, and it will be you if I am burned. My hand grabs your world. The sun shows two faces, two qualities that have been scattered on the other side of a room where we struggle and live. I am that and you are this which is the twofold evolution, the eyes the arms the rhythm the breath and all that my language cannot currently accept.

I am sick with these words that have not the power of another medium where we are content. I am thinking this life death is not what it was. I am going to meet the wall the twins that may be us that may be others. I am aware there is something more terrible. There is a question pulling at you, there is a vacuum pulling at me. There is a moment when we have passed beyond the ordinary gray covers of a world, smoking sulfur immensity of defects, smallness of this room largeness of this circle above laughter tears rain and brains that keep things moving even when the lungs are constricted.

I am here and the cries are not. They are me but they are not here. They are scattered spirits, they are night suspended, they are streams of liquid fire, of love divided. They are a city where each house stands in the same place. They are an island deadened by pain. They are a motive bristling with fury, ageless trembling, not able to end the hunger for a freedom not felt.

We contemplate this sentence in a country filled with mountains which are also echoes that travel from room to room. Many rooms have windows which must be expressed as something else. Many thoughts are what we see through those windows. Many fears are what we do not see through those windows. Many dreams are what would be necessary were we to avoid the determination of those windows.

We look away in one of the rooms. We look away from the windows and we look toward each other. We behold two lives two candles burning in a forest of division, crying laughing searching for an answer surrounded by lies.

This was supposed to be a story of our love, and this was supposed to be a pattern we could recognize. This was supposed to be an area great enough to believe and small enough to grasp. This was supposed to be an ecstasy a tenseness a firmament of full prophetic meaning shining across the night.

I looked back and it seemed I had failed. My thought was incapable of changing for that one moment and that one moment was what I was expressing. There was an explosion which was always almost happening and which has happened, but the moment of its actual occurrence was impossible to touch or feel. That exact moment was never there

and still and yet I know
there was a solution
passing between
us then.

IMPLICIT

None of us were
past dying of the thing unseen.

Here for a moment
that she couldn't believe.

Reeled off like
sunlight in the shadow of
so different as to throw away
more reasonable solitude.

A spirit thinking why
be unhappy with the
fall backwards away from
yesterday's most recent mistake.

Pattern that clarified
what response became
unspeakable at the same time
she failed to overcome
the power of words'
moment of betrayal by words.

There and then
showed the way verging on
edges green by silence.
Cliff shade brought down
more aflame than luminous.

Savage impulse working toward
a life so seldom admitted

within this complication
that she is and we are.

SOMEHOW

Listen to the dead
notes germ swallowed
claim urge, fast protect
blade beneath this
seeming difference

What we show in love
work cited
mark cool branch
and nowhere common
state what channel
always stolen

Such breath, dark damp
fear of losing sleep
for every tired sentence

Not quite first hand
dream wage host
in fog delivered
matter more current

Life still unreal
worship over a line
to roof and answer

Fault use, limb cure
touch speak so to speak
the body rising
back by hidden balance

Ordinary child
to stay alive
change recover
approve corrective
period total
when we don’t belong

LET US KNOW

1.

Who are we to read everything,
crush specific ruling to say what if.

Cause of our confusions outlet or
even mosaic like a sponge.

Participate problem raised to motion,
tumble obsession on toward next.

2.

How it feels walks down maddening
unlike men. Clawing she endures among
other global when diving in bad visibility.

The way love wrinkles a penchant for
pragmatism left free only with hindsight.
Life feelings being connected in some

basic catalogue shipped in to the sick
unplace situated where a token tells me
of the margin that is dangerous direct.

3.

Homage pours flesh word as through
more creatures of difference. Book

of human lives this conduct inhabits.
Letters gone underground just because

the day manages shapes that move
the cover from lands of saga blood.

4.

What falls amid first finger,
whispering mischief in an airy
circle distilled from arrogance.
Sounding shore for the next

child lyric within our view.
Surface not reflection toward
a sequence in love with one
pure chord that is expansion

address most effacing within.
First name first print to mark
belief, to be awake asleep and
lead the art of passing random

bursts of luck. Boundary arms
stretched past the edges being
made and made again, looking
as Egypt through the stench.

SHE BALANCES

for JMB and SEM

Fine attention makes her
so appealing wish.

Key length words set to fit
number or hermetic aura.

Ellipses pronounced
frequency process with

part arbitrary rather like
breaths in a basic contentment.

This sense does not exclude
the first eye visual lines which

are adding a quality about them.
Creates another shape for the

mirror and its stasis/evolution.
Rising hunger suggested and

directed toward an other.
Prayer lying still until each page

becomes light and form which
can be read as a kind present.

Moving emanating quiet self god.
Spree of evanescent

corresponding focus to that other.
Passage integral that addresses

a broader mass culture.
Another kind of double or

multiple in the middle of
fortuitous technique.

Dark circles on about the wish
for things to have meaning.

Release feet, provide
sense of balance as a tool

created by oral and/or
conceptual echoings.

Quiet breeding world from raw
precursor. Stampface scrapbook

pretend indulgence in the
out-take rocks to sleep and

musters a correlative not only
of her most enduring work.

HALO *for JML*

Ridiculous stain rooted thick pillar and
little courage unrecorded.

Perhaps decline runs again, eating anywhere
once despair reached reward rain sighting.

Old attitude surrounded in life specific,
incessant body jealous assembly dancing
into play behind cowardice.

Run fill society ribs, precise shoulders,
fading friends with ordinary horizon anxious.

Together which table which door nailed to
perception waves salute.

Breath cracked darkness, dawn throats
swallow, seek wrinkle where knowing alone
used the range the shore stamped endless.

There rides blood from whirling love,
makes false spread wings of living flow.

Storms night overblown last habit extreme.
Storms red once fronted before other need.

MISSION NORMAL

Circumstance crushed a motive
that is indifferent to ordinary life.
Endless viewpoints trapped
in the frozen powerhouse
of yesterday's imagination.

Photographic likeness knocking
on a wall of blood red mirrors
and the choices they care about.
Anxious image being undercut
at the flick of an unseen switch.

Trouble at the edge
transubstantiated into
a battlefield and uniforms
that cover the current landscape
with a deluge of facts.

Mechanical dynamic pastiche.
Disparate ahistorical response.
Postmythical horizon
turning around forever
in the blind light of nowhere else.

OR SO EMITS

Whose eyes do the activating utterance
with pure vulture archetypes,
stampede across the sky emanating
from an arid impulse poking holes
in hegemonic forces.

We see at face value, using cruder
and rougher methods to keep everyone
deleting, substituting, inserting
a resistance to the strong programme.

We go slavish of praise without
reference to shadows circling overhead.
We are dominated again and again
by dark difference staggered in
ice transformations from other
perturbation forms.

Rainbow to the moon over which
the solid blue spirit bridge
opened its teeth just enough to allow
souls to pass in a charming country.

Not a direction so much as
what we've taken from a better mind
at work. Legacy of systems beyond
an illusion that the author of
successful poems creates.

Monolithic structure more ironic
than the poet's desire to
escape her choice of how an escape
remains dead to those people for whom
poetry is outside or above.

The same is true when someone says
a speaking subject is a fairy tale
learning of love and language and music
in the crevices of everyday activity.

Show of confidence, affection, silliness
in our suspicion of a tradition
that includes nostalgic believing in
contact to evoke a throwback
to the prevalent winds of
distance and analysis.

Not realism but more real roots
of who and what we are among
shared forms of social power gradients.
Awareness built up through experience
at a nodal point of form-making values.

Everyday buzz stretching the site
of writing whose voices disappear
if we believe in a thoroughly exploded
subject. Process that outlines
another hazard in an attempt to
rid the poem of the burden
and desire of the ego.

Objective versus subjective danger
of one particular hegemonic paradigm.
Assay of the distance between
concentration seen as a reader and
the imprint of forces we cannot control.

SMOKE NECESSARY

Detective as curing power to ask severance was I believe when visions occur. Avail mysterious data put in one better position with a particular format. Obtain very old uncultivated day in search of substantial amount. Pose proudly tasted stranger from reputation building almost as the mountains we could not see through a reality making things difficult all around the earth.

Leave ordinary, leave composition by local meaning that called humanity out of primates, that called history out of tribal timeless existence. It's present still on wayward trail of no one, moving around and through entirely other species not granted the status not seen as an official view. Unrelated input unexpected passage in the interface between conquest of dimension of time to which whole mapping itself was a series of dimensions to another.

The issue of contact through rebirth. The issue of rebirth through contact. The current flowing toward potential for falling in love with freedom to discuss bizarre preoccupations, hearts of people sexually polymorphic constrained move to the interior world. Peculiar factors impinging on presence of alien logos in mind of developing release. Culture engineers included in design to take every level of past and future emerging ideal. Reached alarm before service, recognizing no century improvement if only because those modalities would be an object for Western languages. Got the feeling America does strange things at an amazing rate, a novel in felt keeping with the lights very low trouble threat smoke necessary to be a part of the next run.

Hard natural cannot be under the belt for very long. Its exposure seems a challenge to a thousand years with tricks with atoms and time for putting a boulder in place of the open fist. An area determined where traffic would be a problem that we would deny. Where sacrifice would be no different than watching the evening news every night. Where people could realize that their talking brought out the celebrated substance by focusing attention made negative to sail right off the edge.

A lot of stress on the generation picked in prescriptions for sexual connotations. Obsolete millions which might allow the changing of things in the idea from one ending to another. Competition in evolution whose arguments were a unique opportunity. Moment of release failing memory in connection with a teleological bias. Bizarre states followed by a common veneer, transforming people who take a source of gnosis in the voice that spoke to Plato. Immense judgment pressing downward on personal experience. Incredible resource causing chaos in the group monologue. Quality of timing with regard to obligation to be informed as an abuser of the emotions in thick black water.

We argue about this and then we cough up what isn't. We live oblivious and go very close to the neighborhood out of control. Moving beyond history causal division throwing its shadow across a landscape that is totally unique. Forward flow of entropic circumstance onto a sliding filter. Lifelong target never so easy as following someone else's rules. Enterprise of thinking trapped in a world with too much thought as such to fear death and misdirect the humanness of a name.

Where we come from only to be projected in the absence of interaction which appeared much later and became electronic. Unspeakable stands revealed in that moment advertised by a new beginning. The consecration and concatenation rapidly pure plasma not yet cooled. The origin whistling through teeth number familiar with judged vision state. The living in radiance of course not possible, moved by will perhaps by breath without wish to obscure what was expunged through limitations and sincerity from a phase previously considered in some folk belief brought out by today.

Swampy lowland gathered some distance and destroyed by death cures above. Mature green voucher specimens pulling our leg with a joke less fortunate to visit tomorrow out of complaints moving well below the earth. Vehicle of damage that knows the trip reinforced experiments with sound, uncertain as to proceed in the style of chanting from impersonal later agents, completely broke by someone's ever alike network of property extreme.

No means yes in Greek to the impulse supplied to take out novel information. Something connected up in the individual's mind voice which was not associated with moving from one society brought to bear on the news given of what they were saying. Motive rising out of taboo to question the basis of an argument, the grass growing perpendicular narrow corridors, the similar habits identified as time perhaps from land-locked value and insights of a kind pipeline to the presence of the Goddess.

Climate eating desire through ecstatic work crop where lifestyles are the context of modern society. Strike total that is transferred in the silvery appearance and certain forms current which impart an androgynous shape-shifting chance upon the mirror of cultural expectations. Could be drowsy in darkness with eyes closed that cannot be surpassed. Could draw lines worldwide extravagant dream higher logic which disappeared before our coming. Enveloped frozen form of self in the deep down cavern instantly awoke assertion in the way. Unbidden thought brought to crystalline essential thought whipped into fury derived through radiant features, wombs' blood flow living belief in a subject seen as crucial in the early investigation, passing tears shed on the very denial of one who stood hard and fast and decided that our circumstance didn't know what happened.

This would be just a part of the ranges of the deserts of the choral retinue of the generated half-page meaning. This would go in and come out on a level related to the difficulty of moving around future patterns and trends always trying to meld two perspectives. Dark age memory determined in the unreal segments of this sort of thing. A single decision, a time-based providing bridge at every point. A nonprofit foundation of plants that carry the body in native ideas which have never been brought out. A promise dissolving the sleep of walls, guiding experience that changes overnight. A self-reflecting partnership emerging into the light of day: windswept matrix, species of resurrection, cutting edge moving along the surface shape language system inherited to accept the power of endless and terminal in one.

SHOULDER

What battle am I fighting?
What place am I arriving at
when everything I'm aiming at
stands still?

Some idea of me protests so well
this setting magically divided
into three parts which both of us
remember like our life
depended on it.
Some idea fighting back the tears
of any origin that changes
quickly into a book
we want to read but can't.

The lines the words
checking material input flow,
matching waveforms
through predicted incongruities
in the human experience.

A flight of virtues as needed,
the time what trouble
stood in the middle of evidence
I want so badly to follow
with something terrified by
the lower level of my belief system.

The last point the best
and then it changes into some
nameless radical viewpoint
standing by the side of the road
and laughing as I drive by
on my way to another
overpriced resort facility.

I couldn't say I wanted to be here
more or less than its opposite
made life turn around
without considering who was
and wasn't listening.
I couldn't appreciate
the second chance I was given
in exchange for too much
superficial freedom.

Full stop prone before that source,
challenge immediate in which
the power of yesterday
has intensified dreamlike voices
we try but mostly fail to separate
from everything else.

Clouds and light, habit and desire
getting tired moving back and forth,
falling asleep and heading home
on unpaved roads that are older
than the earth.

Arriving just like always
when there's no place left to run.

EXQUISITE

Human landscape no longer haunted
by its actors and their behavior.
Certain language residue of questions
bound to a different expanse.

Peculiar longing which would reconcile
a dream of pure localism.
Intricate amassing harmony faithful to
occasions yet arisen, devoted to

poetic stance and survey of ecosystems.
Real visionary demand for
the singularities of place and work
beyond personal intention.

Movement of a literal immediacy
premised upon community relation.
Force virtue conceived
as the heart of a slow accretion.

Masque given credence by form,
affirming an order beyond truth
in the mirroring of self world questions.
Paradoxes persist in the quickening

perception. Heraclitean depths disrupt
contours or assertions of ritual space,
provoke history as a catalogue of ruins
decentering an imaginary polis.

Claims articulate absence encompassed
by a sacred geography. Necessary doubt
refusing to evade the harder imperatives.
Dark process from the void of plenty.

Dream fullness at time's embrace
of the emptiness that knowledge requires.
Image asserting meaning's immanence,
allowing no chasm between words

and the laws of economy descent.
Primary tensions are seen to conflate
the eternity of such views.
Self dark interiors move toward

an awakening to forms already present.
Imaginative marks defy relations
favored by singling out
this temporal hieratic event.

SILVER BLACK

Less field language of familiar
articulate viscous
heartfelt glow surrounding
force at a relative
discharge boundary
that tries to be enough.

Expected alien foot and thunder
running through the temple
overnight stigma
fundamental myriad
said so much about the part
I may find curious.

Motive set on fire in the very flesh
story escape of projection
furrowed memory dwelling
edge by mirror to imagine
rain or wind not substituted
for something else.

Burst of continuing
gallows music
door uncovered upon the waiting
appendage no longer mistaken
denial the world shown
body manifold to give.

POSSESSION

Tale of wicked dawn
outside image weapon
makes me accomplish
consent ravenous

Narcotic asserting
furtive and vocal
given to like advantage
enduring the day
the mind the house scatter
dark room speech
covenant no way obscure
paradise hollow dream
in suicide past

Strike bulging maze
said generation now
almost sky fear abandon
one another

Eat matter in public intimate
rage stone not look force
within killing words
broken cutting burning
between your millions hidden
and paid for empty

Written with a shut door
spinning faster body
to inhabit when I'm
out in the cold or stuck
in midway country

Put down drop ever wealth
return years' foothold
foreign music lost on
such deep liquid

Heaven sent ground motive
blazing shell street current
hand in the way of desire
becoming helpless

Rain over miracle sign
needle facing inward light
mountain roots of power
finds me more at the start

NO ISLAND

Tangle deep at night of my empty hands.
Attitude scatter, press claims unheard
against the clock. Overwhelm direction,
cast elbow circuit, set face nature to
know I'm stronger for the same old life.

Gone to finish ruins I see everywhere.
One beside me in the troubled oath,
another moving eyes, tempered flames
and cries with the last thought of pain.

Shouting at the world made wrong from
too much wanting. Harvest falter rhythm,
close in sleep I know can only get deeper.
Spread idea forgotten text, endure escape
result of chance, dark trees black breath

under recess counter vigil, bliss grave
siren, broken treaty fear of relic other
native sentence flowing with wind until
it changes and I leave the world alone.